Market Corrections 101: How to protect and grow your investments

CLARA CAPITAL

Contents

I   Understanding Market Corrections

1 Overview   3
2 Definition and Types of Market Corrections   6
3 Factors Influencing Market Corrections   9

II   Historical Market Corrections

4 Overview   15
5 The 1929 Stock Market Crash   18
6 The 1987 Black Monday Crash   20
7 The 1987 Black Monday Crash   23
8 The 2000 Dot-Com Bubble Burst   26
9 The 2008 Financial Crisis   30
10 The 2020 COVID-19 Market Crash   34

III   Impact of Market Corrections

11 Overview   39
12 On Investments   42
13 On Economy   44

IV Strategies to Protect Investments during Market Corrections

14 Overview   49
15 Diversification   52
16 Hedging   54
17 Stop Loss Orders   57

V Strategies to Grow Investments during Market Corrections

18 Overview   63
19 Value Investing   65
20 Dollar-Cost Averaging   68
21 Investing in Defensive Stocks   71

VI Role of Investment Advisors during Market Corrections

22 Overview   77
23 Identifying Investment Opportunities   80
24 Managing Risks   83
25 Developing a Correction-Ready Portfolio   85

VII Psychological Aspects of Market Corrections

26 Overview   91
27 Investor Behavior during Corrections   94
28 Handling Fear and Greed   97
29 Importance of Patience and Discipline   100

VIII   Legal and Regulatory Aspects of Market Corrections

30 Overview   105
31 Government Interventions   109
32 Regulatory Guidelines for Investors   111
33 Legal Rights and Protections for Investors   114

About the Author   117

I

Understanding Market Corrections

1

Overview

Market corrections are a natural part of the financial market cycle, and it is essential for investors to understand their significance and dynamics. In this chapter, we will delve into the topic of market corrections from a beginner's standpoint, exploring what they are, why they occur, and how individuals can protect and even grow their investments during these periods of volatility.

Market corrections refer to temporary declines or reversals in the overall value of the financial market after a period of significant growth. They are often characterized by a decline of at least 10% from recent market highs. While they can evoke fear and uncertainty among investors, it is important to remember that market corrections are a healthy and necessary feature of any market.

The main reasons behind market corrections are multifaceted. They can occur due to various factors such as economic downturns, geopolitical events, changes in government policies, or even a market simply taking a breather after a prolonged period of growth. Whatever the catalyst, market corrections serve as a natural way to balance out excessive optimism, remove overvalued assets, and create opportunities for new investments.

Investors need to have a proactive approach to navigate market corrections effectively. Here are some strategies to consider for protecting and growing investments during these periods:

1. Diversification:

Maintaining a well-diversified investment portfolio spread across different asset classes, sectors, and geographical regions can help mitigate risk during market corrections. By diversifying, investors reduce their exposure to the downturn of any single investment.

2. Long-term perspective:

While market corrections can cause temporary losses, it is essential to maintain a long-term perspective. History has shown that markets tend to recover and reach new highs over time. Staying invested and focusing on long-term goals can help ride out market volatility.

3. Regular investment:

Utilizing a disciplined investment approach, such as dollar-cost averaging, can be effective during market corrections. By investing a fixed amount regularly, investors can take advantage of lower prices, as they buy more shares when markets are down. This strategy helps in reducing the impact of short-term market movements on the overall investment.

4. Fundamental analysis:

Understanding the fundamentals of the investments is vital during market corrections. Examining the financial health, competitive position, and growth prospects of individual companies or assets can enable investors to make informed decisions. Consider investing in quality assets with a history of resilience.

5. Opportunistic buying:

Market corrections offer opportunities to buy quality assets at discounted prices. When stocks or other investments experience widespread declines, it may be an opportune time to consider adding to the portfolio or initiating new positions. However, thorough research and careful consideration of each investment are crucial.

6. Risk management:

Implementing risk management techniques is essential during market corrections. Setting stop-loss orders, which trigger automatic selling if an investment reaches a certain price level, can help limit potential losses. This strategy allows investors to protect themselves from further declines while preserving capital.

7. Seek professional advice:

Market corrections can be complex, and seeking guidance from qualified financial professionals can provide valuable insights. Financial advisors and investment experts can assist in developing personalized strategies and offer reassurance during volatile market conditions.

Remember, market corrections are an inherent part of investing, and successful investors navigate through these downturns with a well-thought-out plan. By diversifying, maintaining a long-term perspective, conducting thorough research, and implementing risk management techniques, individuals can protect and potentially grow their investments during market corrections.

2

Definition and Types of Market Corrections

Definition:

A market correction occurs when stock prices decline by at least 10% from their recent peak, resulting in a temporary downturn in the overall market. While it can lead to brief periods of panic and uncertainty, market corrections are a natural and healthy part of the market cycle, offering opportunities for investors to reassess their portfolios and make disciplined investment decisions.

Types of Market Corrections:

Market corrections can be classified into three distinct types, each with its own characteristics:

1. Pullback:

A pullback is the mildest form of market correction, typically resulting in a decline of around 5-10% from recent highs. Pullbacks are short-lived, lasting for just a few weeks to a few months, and are often considered healthy corrections within an ongoing bull market. Investors generally view pullbacks as buying opportunities rather than reasons to panic.

2. Correction:

A correction is a more significant market decline, ranging from 10% to 20% below recent peaks. Corrections can last several months and are marked by increased market volatility. Although they may induce fear and anxiety, corrections are often followed by new highs as investors evaluate their positions and seek undervalued opportunities.

3. Bear Market:

A bear market represents a sustained and significant decline in stock prices, typically exceeding 20%. Bear markets may last for months or even years, and investor sentiment becomes pessimistic. During this period, economic indicators worsen, and fear dominates the market. Investors must exercise caution during bear markets, as they can be particularly challenging for long-term wealth accumulation.

Protecting and Growing Investments During Market Corrections:

1. Diversify Your Portfolio:

Spreading investments across various asset classes and sectors can help cushion the impact of market corrections.

2. Regularly Rebalance:

Periodically reassess your portfolio's asset allocation, selling overvalued assets and purchasing undervalued ones to maintain a balanced portfolio.

3. Adopt a Long-Term Perspective:

Don't let short-term market movements dictate your investment decisions. Stay focused on long-term financial goals.

4. Stay Informed:

Continuously educate yourself about market trends and economic indicators to make informed investment choices.

5. Consider Professional Advice:

Consulting a financial advisor can provide valuable insights and tailor strategies to your specific investment needs.

3

Factors Influencing Market Corrections

Factors Influencing Market Corrections:

1. Economic Fundamentals:

Economic factors play a crucial role in driving market corrections. These may include a slowdown in economic growth, rising interest rates, inflationary pressures, or geopolitical tensions. Negative economic indicators can trigger investor concerns, leading to a correction.

2. Investor Sentiment:

Greed and fear are common emotions that heavily influence market behavior. During a bull market, investor euphoria can drive prices to unsustainable levels, creating an environment ripe for a correction. Conversely, panic and sell-offs during a bear market can exacerbate the magnitude of the correction.

3. Valuation Metrics:

Overvaluation of assets is a significant factor that can contribute to market corrections. When market prices surpass the intrinsic value of assets, it creates an imbalance that is likely to be rectified through a correction.

4. Sector Rotation:

Shifts in investor preferences among sectors can trigger market corrections. For example, if investors decide to move from growth-oriented stocks to more defensive sectors, it can result in an overall downward movement in the market.

5. Market Manipulation:

Though uncommon, market manipulations or unexpected exogenous factors can influence corrections. Instances such as fraud, insider trading, or unexpected large trading activities can disrupt market stability.

Protecting and Growing Investments during Market Corrections:

1. Diversification:

Building a diversified portfolio helps mitigate the impact of market corrections. By spreading investments across various asset classes, sectors, and geographic regions, investors can reduce the risk associated with a single investment or market segment.

2. Asset Allocation:

Strategic asset allocation involves determining the optimal distribution across different asset classes, such as stocks, bonds, real estate, and commodities. This approach allows investors to balance risk and return potential, providing protection during market corrections.

3. Risk Management:

Implementing risk management strategies, such as setting stop-loss orders or employing hedging techniques, can limit potential losses during market downturns.

4. Long-Term Perspective:

Maintaining a long-term investment approach can help investors ride out market corrections without making impulsive decisions. Studies have shown that attempting to time the market often leads to suboptimal returns.

5. Fundamental Analysis:

Conducting thorough research and analyzing the intrinsic value of investments can help identify undervalued opportunities and avoid overvalued assets that may be susceptible to corrections.

II

Historical Market Corrections

4

Overview

Historical market corrections play a fundamental role in the financial world. They refer to periods in which the stock market experiences a significant decline after a prolonged period of growth. These corrections are part of the natural cycle of market fluctuations, and understanding them is crucial for investors, analysts, and financial professionals. This chapter will provide a simple and comprehensive understanding of historical market corrections, including their causes, impacts, and important examples.

Causes of Historical Market Corrections:

1. Economic Factors:

Market corrections can be triggered by various economic factors such as recessions, rising interest rates, inflation, or an economic bubble bursting.

2. Investor Sentiment:

Investor psychology also plays a role in market corrections. Fear, panic, and uncertainty can lead to a selling spree, causing prices to drop.

3. External Events:

Geopolitical tensions, wars, natural disasters, or unexpected global events can create volatility in the market, leading to corrections.

Impacts of Historical Market Corrections:

1. Wealth Implications:

Market corrections can lead to significant wealth erosion for investors, especially those heavily invested in stocks or equity-based securities.

2. Consumer Confidence:

A declining stock market might affect consumer confidence, resulting in reduced spending and decreased economic activity.

3. Job Market:

During market corrections, businesses may face financial challenges, leading to lay-offs and a weakened job market.

4. Investor Behavior:

Historical market corrections can instill cautious behavior among investors, leading to a shift in investment strategies and long-term decision-making.

Important Examples of Historical Market Corrections:

1. The Great Depression (1929):

This was one of the most severe market corrections in history triggered by the Wall Street crash, leading to a prolonged economic downturn worldwide.

2. Dot-com Bubble Burst (2000):

The rapid burst of the dot-com bubble resulted in a significant correction, leading to a decline in many technology-focused stocks.

3. Global Financial Crisis (2008):

The collapse of the subprime mortgage market in the United States caused a global financial crisis, resulting in a sharp correction in global stock markets.

Lessons from Historical Market Corrections:

1. Diversification and Risk Management:

Historical market corrections highlight the importance of diversifying investment portfolios and having a risk management strategy in place.

2. Long-Term Perspective:

Understanding that market corrections are temporary and markets tend to recover over time guides investors to maintain a long-term perspective.

3. Emotional Control:

Avoiding emotional decision-making, such as panic selling during a correction, is vital for investors aiming to maximize returns.

Conclusion:

Historical market corrections are integral parts of the financial landscape, impacting investors, businesses, and economies. Learning from these corrections helps investors navigate through market volatility, minimize losses, and make informed decisions. By understanding the causes, impacts, and examples of historical market corrections, individuals can build a resilient investment strategy and approach market fluctuations with confidence.

5

The 1929 Stock Market Crash

One of the most significant historical market corrections occurred during the 1929 stock market crash. This event had a profound impact on the global economy, leading to the Great Depression. Understanding the causes, consequences, and lessons learned from the 1929 stock market crash is crucial for comprehending market corrections and their implications.

Causes:

The 1929 stock market crash was caused by a combination of economic factors. Over the preceding years, the stock market experienced substantial growth, fueled by speculative buying and excessive optimism. This exuberance led to inflated stock prices, detached from their underlying value. Additionally, unsound trading practices, such as buying stocks on margin (borrowed money), further inflated the market. The crash was triggered when confidence began to wane, and investors rushed to sell their stocks, causing a domino effect of falling prices.

Consequences:

The consequences of the 1929 stock market crash were devastating and widespread. The crash precipitated the Great Depression, a severe economic downturn that lasted until the late 1930s. The market crash wiped out billions of dollars in wealth, leading to massive job losses, business failures, and a decline in consumer spending. Banks and financial institutions collapsed, contributing to a deepening economic crisis. Unemployment rates soared, poverty levels rose, and social unrest became prevalent. The crash had a global impact, exacerbating existing economic weaknesses in other countries.

Lessons Learned:

The 1929 stock market crash taught valuable lessons that have shaped financial systems and regulations since then. One of the key takeaways was the importance of monitoring and controlling speculative behavior in the market. Governments implemented stricter regulations to prevent excessive speculation and introduce transparency in trading practices. Additionally, the crash highlighted the necessity of comprehensive economic policies to prevent and mitigate financial crises. Central banks were established or strengthened to provide stability and liquidity to the financial system. Governments prioritized measures to protect banks, ensuring their solvency and averting further economic collapses. The crash also emphasized the significance of diversified investment strategies to reduce risk and promote long-term stability.

Conclusion:

The 1929 stock market crash serves as a stark reminder of the potential conse-quences of unchecked speculative behavior and market exuberance. It was a pivotal event in global financial history, leading to the Great Depression and shaping subsequent economic policies and regulations. Understanding this historical market correction provides valuable insights into the importance of monitoring markets, implementing prudent investment strategies, and establishing robust financial systems to prevent disruptive crises. By studying historical market corrections, we learn from past mistakes to foster a more stable and resilient financial environment.

6

The 1987 Black Monday Crash

Another significant event in financial history is the "Black Monday" of 1987. This chapter will delve into the aspects and impacts of the historical market correction that occurred during this time, providing insights into the causes, consequences, and lessons learned from the 1987 Black Monday.

Background:

The Black Monday correction took place on October 19, 1987, in the United States and had a ripple effect on global financial markets. It is considered one of the largest single-day market crashes in history. Prior to this event, the stock market experienced substantial growth throughout the early and mid-1980s. However, the market was becoming increasingly overvalued due to speculative behavior, a growing reliance on computerized trading, and concerns over international trade imbalances.

Causes:

Several factors contributed to the 1987 market correction. One key element was the prevalent use of computerized trading systems, known as program trading or portfolio insurance. These systems were designed to automatically execute trades based on predetermined algorithms and strategies. However, on Black Monday, these trading programs exacerbated the market decline as they triggered a wave of selling when certain predetermined price levels were breached.

Additionally, economic concerns, such as the growing U.S. trade deficit and political tensions between the United States and Middle Eastern countries, added to the existing apprehensions. As uncertainty grew, fear-driven mass selling intensified, leading to a widespread panic and a collapse in stock prices.

Consequences:

The immediate consequences of the 1987 Black Monday market correction were severe. On that day alone, the Dow Jones Industrial Average (DJIA) plummeted by approximately 22%, wiping out billions of dollars in market value. The effects of this crash were not limited to the United States; international markets also experienced significant declines.

However, despite the magnitude of the crash, the long-term consequences were relatively limited. Unlike the Great Depression in the 1930s, the economy did not spiral into a prolonged recession or depression. Within a couple of years, the stock market regained its previous levels, as the underlying economic fundamentals remained strong.

Lessons learned:

The 1987 market correction led to several important lessons and subsequent reforms within the financial industry. Regulators realized the need for greater oversight to prevent excessive speculation and to ensure market stability. As a result, circuit breakers were implemented to halt trading temporarily if market declines exceed certain thresholds. These measures aimed to prevent extreme panic selling.

Another significant outcome was the recognition of the importance of understanding and managing the impact of algorithmic or computerized trading systems. This event prompted regulators and market participants to develop more nuanced risk management strategies, including stress-testing and better control mechanisms for these automated systems.

Conclusion:

The 1987 Black Monday market correction serves as a stark reminder of the vulnerability of financial markets to unpredictable events and herd behavior. It highlighted the need for improved regulation, risk management practices, and investor education to prevent market disruptions. While the immediate consequences were severe, the incident did not have long-lasting negative effects on the overall economy, as measures were implemented to address the underlying causes of the crash. Understanding historical market corrections, such as the 1987 Black Monday, helps investors and policymakers better prepare for future market downturns, fostering a more stable and resilient financial system.

7

The 1987 Black Monday Crash

Another significant event in financial history is the "Black Monday" of 1987. This chapter will delve into the aspects and impacts of the historical market correction that occurred during this time, providing insights into the causes, consequences, and lessons learned from the 1987 Black Monday.

Background:

The Black Monday correction took place on October 19, 1987, in the United States and had a ripple effect on global financial markets. It is considered one of the largest single-day market crashes in history. Prior to this event, the stock market experienced substantial growth throughout the early and mid-1980s. However, the market was becoming increasingly overvalued due to speculative behavior, a growing reliance on computerized trading, and concerns over international trade imbalances.

Causes:

Several factors contributed to the 1987 market correction. One key element was the prevalent use of computerized trading systems, known as program trading or portfolio insurance. These systems were designed to automatically execute trades based on predetermined algorithms and strategies. However, on Black Monday, these trading programs exacerbated the market decline as they triggered a wave of selling when certain predetermined price levels were breached.

Additionally, economic concerns, such as the growing U.S. trade deficit and political tensions between the United States and Middle Eastern countries, added to the existing apprehensions. As uncertainty grew, fear-driven mass selling intensified, leading to a widespread panic and a collapse in stock prices.

Consequences:

The immediate consequences of the 1987 Black Monday market correction were severe. On that day alone, the Dow Jones Industrial Average (DJIA) plummeted by approximately 22%, wiping out billions of dollars in market value. The effects of this crash were not limited to the United States; international markets also experienced significant declines.

However, despite the magnitude of the crash, the long-term consequences were relatively limited. Unlike the Great Depression in the 1930s, the economy did not spiral into a prolonged recession or depression. Within a couple of years, the stock market regained its previous levels, as the underlying economic fundamentals remained strong.

Lessons learned:

The 1987 market correction led to several important lessons and subsequent reforms within the financial industry. Regulators realized the need for greater oversight to prevent excessive speculation and to ensure market stability. As a result, circuit breakers were implemented to halt trading temporarily if market declines exceed certain thresholds. These measures aimed to prevent extreme panic selling.

Another significant outcome was the recognition of the importance of understanding and managing the impact of algorithmic or computerized trading systems. This event prompted regulators and market participants to develop more nuanced risk management strategies, including stress-testing and better control mechanisms for these automated systems.

Conclusion:

The 1987 Black Monday market correction serves as a stark reminder of the vulnerability of financial markets to unpredictable events and herd behavior. It highlighted the need for improved regulation, risk management practices, and investor education to prevent market disruptions. While the immediate consequences were severe, the incident did not have long-lasting negative effects on the overall economy, as measures were implemented to address the underlying causes of the crash. Understanding historical market corrections, such as the 1987 Black Monday, helps investors and policymakers better prepare for future market downturns, fostering a more stable and resilient financial system.

8

The 2000 Dot-Com Bubble Burst

Another notable example of a market correction is the dot-com bubble burst in the early 2000s, which had a significant impact on the global economy and stock market.

Overview:

The dot-com bubble refers to the rapid rise and subsequent fall in the value of internet-based companies from the late 1990s to early 2000s. During this period, the valuations of internet-based companies skyrocketed, fueled by investor enthusiasm and speculation. However, this excessive valuation was often detached from the companies' actual financial performance and earnings potential. Eventually, the bubble burst, leading to a significant market correction.

Causes of the Dot-Com Bubble:

1. Investor Over-Enthusiasm:

During the late 1990s, investors were captivated by the potential of the internet and its transformative impact on commerce. Companies with little or no profits were valued at astronomical levels as investors chased high-growth opportunities.

2. Speculation and Irrational Exuberance:

Many investors bought stocks solely based on the expectation that others would buy them at higher prices in the future. This speculative behavior drove stock prices to unsustainable levels.

3. Lack of Fundamental Analysis:

Traditional valuation metrics, such as price-to-earnings ratios, were often disregarded during this period. Investors focused more on the potential of the internet rather than the actual financial performance of companies.

4. Misguided Business Models:

Many dot-com companies had business models that were untested or unsustainable in the long run. Several of these companies had huge losses and were unable to generate significant revenues.

Bubble Burst and Market Correction:

The bursting of the dot-com bubble began in early 2000 and had a profound impact on the market. As investors started to question the sustainability of these overvalued companies, a significant sell-off commenced. Stock prices plummeted, leading to a market correction.

1. Sharp Decline in Stock Prices:

From March 2000 to October 2002, the NASDAQ Composite Index, heavily influenced by technology companies, lost nearly 80% of its value. Many dot-com companies went bankrupt, and investors suffered substantial losses.

2. Investor Confidence Erosion:

The burst of the dot-com bubble eroded investor confidence in the stock market, resulting in a broader market correction that affected various sectors beyond technology.

3. Impact on the Economy:

The bursting of the dot-com bubble had a significant impact on the overall economy. Massive layoffs occurred in the technology sector, and consumer spending decreased, contributing to an economic slowdown.

Lessons Learned:

1. Valuation Matters:

The dot-com bubble bust highlights the importance of evaluating companies based on their fundamental financials rather than speculative hype.

2. Diversification:

Investors learned the importance of diversifying their portfolios across different sectors, asset classes, and geographical regions to mitigate the impact of market corrections.

3. Long-Term Perspective:

The dot-com bubble serves as a reminder that markets go through cycles, and it's essential to maintain a long-term perspective and not get caught up in short-term market volatility.

Conclusion:

The dot-com bubble burst in the early 2000s represents a significant historical market correction that resulted from investor over-enthusiasm, speculation, and unrealistic valuations of dot-com companies. The burst had profound impacts on the stock market, economy, and investor confidence. A careful study of historical market corrections like the dot-com bubble burst helps us gain insights to avoid similar mistakes in the future and navigate market volatility more effectively.

9

The 2008 Financial Crisis

Another notable historical market correction is the 2008 financial crisis, which had a significant impact on the global economy. This chapter provides a comprehensive look at the 2008 financial crisis, its causes, repercussions, and lessons learned.

Causes of the 2008 Financial Crisis:

The 2008 financial crisis was caused by a combination of factors that created a perfect storm in the global financial system. Some key causes include:

1. Subprime Mortgage Crisis:

The crisis originated in the United States with the collapse of the subprime mortgage market. Risky lending practices, including issuing mortgages to borrowers with poor creditworthiness, led to a housing bubble that eventually burst.

2. Financial Derivatives:

Complex financial instruments, such as mortgage-backed securities and collateralized debt obligations (CDOs), were bundled and sold to investors, spreading the risk throughout the financial system. When the underlying mortgages defaulted, these derivatives faced substantial losses, triggering a domino effect.

3. Excessive Leverage:

Financial institutions had taken on excessive levels of debt, often relying on short-term borrowing to fund their long-term investments. When the crisis hit, the lack of liquidity made it difficult for many institutions to meet their obligations, causing panic and a further deterioration of financial stability.

Repercussions of the Crisis:

The 2008 financial crisis had profound consequences on a global scale, affecting various aspects of the economy and society:

1. Global Economic Recession:

The crisis led to a severe worldwide economic downturn, characterized by reduced economic growth, rising unemployment rates, and declining consumer and business confidence. Many countries faced recessionary conditions, with the impact being particularly severe in the United States and Europe.

2. Bank Failures and Bailouts:

Numerous financial institutions faced insolvency, resulting in significant bank failures. Governments intervened by providing bailouts to troubled banks to prevent a complete collapse of the financial system.

3. Housing Market Collapse:

The crisis caused a sharp drop in housing prices, leaving many homeowners underwater on their mortgages (owed more than the value of their homes). Foreclosures surged, leading to a housing market collapse.

4. Widening Income Inequality:

The crisis widened the wealth gap, as those in lower income brackets were disproportionately affected by job losses and housing market deterioration. This highlighted the systemic inequalities within financial systems.

5. Regulatory Reforms:

The crisis exposed regulatory deficiencies and led to significant reforms worldwide. Governments enacted stricter regulations on financial institutions, aimed at enhancing transparency, reducing risk-taking behavior, and strengthening oversight.

Lessons Learned:

The 2008 financial crisis served as a wake-up call for policymakers, investors, and individuals alike. Some valuable lessons learned from this crisis include:

1. The Importance of Risk Management:

Effective risk management practices, both at the institutional and individual level, are crucial to avoid excessive exposure to market vulnerabilities.

2. Need for Strong Regulatory Oversight:

Governments and regulatory bodies must have robust oversight and monitoring mechanisms in place to identify potential financial risks and to intervene promptly when necessary.

3. The Role of Transparency:

Transparent financial reporting and disclosure practices are vital to ensure investors have access to accurate information to make well-informed decisions.

4. Diversification and Resilience:

Investors should diversify their portfolios, spreading risks across different asset classes and geographies. A diversified portfolio can help alleviate the negative impacts of market corrections.

Conclusion:

The 2008 financial crisis was a significant historical market correction that shook the global economy to its core. It was caused by a combination of factors, primarily stemming from risky lending practices and excessive leverage within the financial system. The repercussions of the crisis were far-reaching and led to a devastating global recession. However, valuable lessons were learned, resulting in regulatory reforms, improvements in risk management practices, and heightened awareness of the importance of transparency and diversification.

10

The 2020 COVID-19 Market Crash

The COVID-19 pandemic had a profound impact on global financial markets, leading to one of the most significant market corrections in recent history. In this chapter, we will delve into the context of the 2020 COVID-19 market crash, examining its causes, consequences, and historical market corrections as a whole.

Causes of the COVID-19 Market Crash:

The COVID-19 market crash can be primarily attributed to the rapid spread of the novel coronavirus and the subsequent lockdown measures implemented by governments globally. These measures aimed to contain the virus but had severe economic repercussions. Industries such as travel, tourism, hospitality, and retail were hit particularly hard, leading to a domino effect across global markets.

The Consequences of the COVID-19 Market Crash:

The COVID-19 market crash had far-reaching consequences, impacting economies, governments, industries, and individual investors. Some of the prominent consequences include:

1. Economic Recession:

The market crash deepened the global recession that began in early 2020. With businesses shutting down, unemployment soared, leading to reduced consumer spending and economic contraction.

2. Volatile Financial Markets:

The crash resulted in heightened market volatility, characterized by wild swings in stock prices, increased trading volumes, and uncertainty among investors. This volatility persisted throughout the pandemic.

3. High-Profile Corporate Bankruptcies:

Several prominent companies, including renowned retailers and airlines, filed for bankruptcy due to the severe economic downturn and their inability to sustain operations amidst the crisis.

4. Government Interventions:

Governments worldwide stepped in with fiscal stimulus packages and monetary measures to mitigate the economic impact. Central banks reduced interest rates, initiated quantitative easing, and injected liquidity into financial markets.

5. Investment Opportunities:

Market corrections create investment opportunities for savvy investors. While many stocks declined during the crash, some sectors, such as technology or healthcare, experienced significant growth. Identifying these opportunities requires careful analysis and understanding of market corrections throughout history.

In conclusion, the 2020 COVID-19 market crash served as a notable historical market correction, triggered by a global pandemic and resulting in significant economic consequences. By studying historical market corrections, investors can gain valuable knowledge to navigate future market uncertainties, identify investment opportunities, and improve decision-making in the world of finance.

III

Impact of Market Corrections

11

Overview

Understanding the impact of market corrections is crucial for investors looking to protect and grow their investments. Market corrections refer to the temporary decline in stock prices, resulting in a decrease of at least 10% from prior highs. While they can be unsettling, market corrections are a normal part of the economic cycle. This chapter will delve into the various aspects of market corrections, including their causes, potential consequences, and strategies to safeguard and enhance your investments.

Causes of Market Corrections:

1. Overvaluation:

Market corrections often occur when stocks become overvalued, surpassing their realistic intrinsic value, which can lead to a correction to more reasonable levels.

2. Economic Factors:

Economic recessions or slowdowns, changes in interest rates, policy decisions, or geopolitical events can trigger market corrections, affecting investor sentiment.

3. Speculative Behavior:

Excessive speculation or "bubbles" within certain sectors can inflate stock prices to unsustainable levels, leading to subsequent corrections.

Consequences of Market Corrections:

1. Psychological Impact:

Market corrections can instill fear and panic among investors, potentially leading to hasty decision-making and irrational behavior.

2. Decreased Portfolio Value:

Stock market corrections typically result in temporary losses in portfolio value, impacting individual stocks, mutual funds, and indexes.

3. Market Volatility:

Corrections can introduce increased market volatility, potentially causing short-term fluctuations that impact both experienced and novice investors.

Protecting and Growing Your Investments:

1. Diversification:

Maintaining a diversified portfolio across various asset classes, sectors, and geographical regions can help mitigate the impact of market corrections on your investments.

2. Asset Allocation:

Allocating your investments across different asset classes such as stocks, bonds, real estate, and cash can provide a cushion during market corrections.

3. Long-term Perspective:

Adopting a long-term investment strategy and avoiding panic-selling can help weather market volatility and allow your investments to recover over time.

4. Investing in Quality:

Focusing on high-quality companies with strong fundamentals, solid track records, and competitive advantages can minimize the impact of market corrections.

5. Analyzing Risk Tolerance:

Assessing and understanding your risk tolerance is crucial in determining an investment strategy that aligns with your ability to handle market fluctuations without compromising your financial goals.

Conclusion:

Market corrections can unnerve investors, but they are a natural part of the market cycle. It is important to understand the causes and consequences of market corrections to protect and grow your investments effectively. Implementing strategies such as diversification, asset allocation, maintaining a long-term perspective, and investing in quality can help mitigate the impact of market corrections, enhance your investment portfolio, and position you for long-term success. Always consult with a financial advisor or professional to tailor an investment plan that aligns with your specific financial situation and goals.

12

On Investments

First and foremost, it is crucial to recognize that market corrections are typically temporary and represent potential buying opportunities rather than a reason to panic. Investors who understand this fundamental concept can navigate market corrections more effectively. During a correction, stock prices may exhibit significant volatility, experiencing sharp declines before eventually rebounding.

One of the key impacts of market corrections on investments lies in the temporary decline in the overall value of a portfolio. This decline can be unnerving for some investors, particularly those who are new to investing. However, it is important to view this as a short-term setback rather than a permanent loss. Investors who maintain a long-term perspective and remain patient often benefit from the recovery that follows a market correction.

It is worth noting that the impact of market corrections varies depending on the investor's asset allocation. Diversification across various asset classes, such as stocks, bonds, and alternative investments, can help mitigate the effects of market corrections. Investors with a well-diversified portfolio may experience smaller declines during market corrections.

Another important impact to consider is the emotional aspect of market corrections. Corrections can create fear and uncertainty among investors, potentially leading to impulsive decision-making. Emotions such as panic selling can result in significant losses if investors sell their holdings during a down market. Maintaining a disciplined investment strategy and avoiding emotional reactions is crucial to weathering market corrections effectively.

Furthermore, market corrections can also present opportunities for investors to identify undervalued stocks or investment opportunities. During a correction, certain sectors or industries may be disproportionately affected, creating potential bargains for savvy investors. Conducting thorough research and analysis can help identify companies that may have been oversold during a correction, offering attractive entry points for long-term growth.

To protect investments during market corrections, diversification, as mentioned earlier, is essential. Diversifying across different asset classes and geographies helps spread risk and reduce the impact of a single market's correction. Additionally, having a well-defined investment plan that aligns with one's financial goals and risk tolerance is crucial. Reviewing and rebalancing the portfolio periodically can ensure that the allocation remains suitable for changing market conditions.

In summary, understanding the impact of market corrections on investments is vital for investors looking to protect and grow their portfolios. Market corrections are temporary setbacks that can create emotional distress and declining portfolio values. However, viewing them as buying opportunities, maintaining a long-term perspective, and staying disciplined can help investors weather market volatility. Diversification, research, and a well-defined investment plan are key elements for successfully navigating market corrections and positioning oneself for long-term investment success.

13

On Economy

Market corrections play a significant role in shaping the economy and can have a substantial impact on investments and overall financial well-being. Understanding these corrections and effectively navigating them is crucial for investors who aim to protect and grow their investments. In this chapter, we will explore the concept of market corrections and examine their effects on the economy.

1. Understanding Market Corrections:

A market correction refers to a temporary decline in stock prices, typically ranging from 10% to 20%, after a significant and sustained increase. While market corrections can be triggered by various factors, they are often driven by investor sentiment, economic conditions, geopolitical events, or simply market cycles. Corrections are a natural and healthy part of a market's functioning, providing an opportunity for the market to readjust and seek a more reasonable valuation.

2. Causes of Market Corrections:

2.1 Investor Sentiment: Investor emotions, such as fear and greed, can play a role in market corrections, as they often trigger overbuying or overselling, leading to price imbalances.

2.2 Economic Factors: Shifts in economic indicators, such as interest rates, inflation, GDP growth, or industry-specific developments, can cause market corrections.

2.3 Geopolitical Events: Political instability, international conflicts, or trade disputes may create uncertainties that spook investors, resulting in market corrections.

2.4 Market Cycles: Periodic market correction is an inherent part of market cycles, which typically consist of bull (growth) and bear (contraction) phases.

3. Effects of Market Corrections on the Economy:

3.1 Investor Confidence: Market corrections can erode investor confidence, leading to more cautious spending behavior, reduced investments, and a slowdown in economic activity.

3.2 Housing Market: A significant drop in stock prices due to a market correction can influence housing markets, affecting mortgage rates, home values, and the overall stability of the real estate industry.

3.3 Consumer Spending: As people witness a decline in their investment portfolios during market corrections, they may cut back on discretionary spending, leading to a decrease in consumer demand.

3.4 Unemployment: Economic slowdowns resulting from market corrections can impact employment rates, as companies may reduce hiring or even implement layoffs to navigate through uncertainties.

3.5 Business Investment: Market corrections often deter businesses from making long-term investments or expansions, as they may adopt a more conservative approach to preserve capital and weather the downturn.

4. Protecting and Growing Investments during Market Corrections:

4.1 Portfolio Diversification: Diversify your investment portfolio across different asset classes and regions to mitigate the impact of a single market correction on your overall holdings.

4.2 Risk Management: Utilize risk management strategies such as setting stop-loss limits, regularly reviewing asset allocations, and maintaining an emergency fund to ensure financial stability during market corrections.

4.3 Long-Term Approach: Adopt a long-term investment strategy rather than attempting to time the market, as historical data suggests that the market generally recovers and provides positive returns over extended periods.

4.4 Seek Professional Advice: Engage with financial advisors or experts who can help assess your risk tolerance, provide guidance on asset allocation, and offer strategies tailored to market conditions.

Conclusion:

Market corrections are an integral part of financial markets, serving as necessary adjustments that maintain market health. Understanding the impact of market corrections on the economy is crucial for protecting and growing investments. By diversifying portfolios, managing risks, adopting a long-term approach, and seeking professional advice, investors can navigate market corrections successfully and turn them into opportunities for growth.

IV

Strategies to Protect Investments during Market Corrections

14

Overview

Market corrections are an inevitable part of financial markets, creating volatility and potential risks for investors. Understanding how to protect investments during periods of market downturns is crucial for safeguarding valuables and maximizing long-term growth. This chapter will provide a simple and extensive overview of the strategies that can be employed to protect investments during market corrections.

1. Diversification:

Diversification is a fundamental technique that helps reduce risk by spreading investments across various asset classes, industries, and regions. By holding a well-diversified portfolio, investors can mitigate the impact of market fluctuations on their holdings. Diversification ensures that the losses from one investment can be offset by gains from other components of the portfolio, thereby minimizing the overall impact of market corrections.

2. Asset Allocation:

Asset allocation refers to the process of distributing investments among different asset classes, such as stocks, bonds, cash, and real estate. A well-balanced asset allocation strategy helps ensure that investments are not overly concentrated in one area, thus reducing vulnerability to market corrections. Asset allocation should be based on an individual's risk tolerance, investment goals, and timeframe.

3. Stop-Loss Orders:

Stop-loss orders are an effective risk management tool that investors can use to protect themselves in the event of a market downturn. By setting a predetermined price at which to sell a particular investment, investors can limit potential losses. Stop-loss orders help prevent emotional decision-making during market corrections, providing a disciplined approach to protect investments.

4. Dollar-Cost Averaging:

Dollar-cost averaging involves investing a fixed amount of money at regular intervals, regardless of market conditions. By consistently buying assets at predetermined intervals, investors reduce the risk of making large investments at the wrong time. This strategy takes advantage of market fluctuations, allowing investors to buy more shares when prices are low and fewer shares when prices are high.

5. Defensive Investment Strategies:

During market corrections, defensive investment strategies can help protect investments from significant losses. These strategies involve shifting investments toward less volatile sectors, such as defensive stocks (companies providing essential goods and services), bonds, or defensive sectors like healthcare and utilities. Defensive investments are relatively more stable during market downturns and can act as a cushion against severe losses.

6. Maintain a Long-Term Perspective:

One of the most critical strategies to protect investments during market corrections is to maintain a long-term perspective. Markets tend to recover over time, and knee-jerk reactions to short-term fluctuations can often result in missed opportunities. Staying focused on investment goals and avoiding panic selling can help investors ride out market downturns and take advantage of subsequent rebounds.

Conclusion:

Market corrections are an integral part of investing, and being prepared for them is crucial for protecting and growing investments. Employing a combination of diversification, asset allocation, stop-loss orders, dollar-cost averaging, defensive investment strategies, and maintaining a long-term perspective can help investors weather market downturns successfully. It is essential to remember that market corrections present opportunities for those who are patient and disciplined, as historical evidence has shown that markets typically recover and continue to grow over the long run.

15

Diversification

Diversification involves spreading your investments across different asset classes, industries, and geographic regions. The goal is to reduce risk by not putting all your eggs in one basket. A well-diversified portfolio can be helpful in weathering market turbulence because not all investments will be affected in the same way. If one sector or asset class is experiencing a downturn, others may be performing well, offsetting potential losses.

There are several ways to diversify your investments. Firstly, you can allocate your funds across different asset classes, such as stocks, bonds, real estate, commodities, and cash equivalents. Each asset class has its own risk and return characteristics, and their performances often differ during market corrections.

Furthermore, diversification can be extended to within the stock market itself. Investing in stocks of different companies from various industries can mitigate the impact of a market correction on your portfolio. This approach recognizes that different sectors may respond differently to market fluctuations due to their unique dynamics and varying levels of sensitivity to economic conditions.

Geographic diversification is another essential aspect of safeguarding your investments. By investing internationally, you can reduce the risks associated with focusing solely on one country's economic performance. It enables you to benefit from the growth potential of different regions while potentially offsetting any negative impacts from a domestic market correction.

Asset allocation is closely linked to diversification. Depending on your risk tolerance and investment goals, you should establish an appropriate mix of assets to create a well-diversified portfolio. Regularly reviewing and rebalancing your portfolio can help maintain the desired asset allocation, ensuring it aligns with your changing financial circumstances and market conditions.

Moreover, diversification does not only apply to traditional investment vehicles. You can also explore alternative investments, such as hedge funds, private equity, or investment in startups, to diversify your portfolio further. These alternatives often have low correlations with traditional investments and can potentially provide greater returns during market corrections.

Lastly, it is crucial to exercise patience and discipline during market corrections. Emotional reactions to market volatility may lead to impulsive decisions that can harm your long-term investment strategy. Staying focused on your goals, sticking to your diversification plan, and seeking professional advice from financial advisors can help you navigate market corrections successfully.

In conclusion, diversification serves as a fundamental strategy for protecting and growing investments during market corrections. Spreading investments across different asset classes, industries, and regions can help mitigate risk and reduce the impact of potential losses. By maintaining a well-diversified portfolio, regularly reviewing asset allocation, and exercising patience, investors can increase their chances of weathering market turbulence and achieving long-term investment success.

16

Hedging

Hedging is an investment strategy used to reduce or offset the risk of adverse price movements in an asset or portfolio. It involves taking an opposing position to an existing investment to minimize potential losses. Hedging allows investors to protect their portfolios during market downturns while maintaining exposure to potential upside opportunities.

Various Hedging Techniques:

1. Traditional Hedging:

This entails diversifying your investment portfolio across different asset classes such as stocks, bonds, cash, and commodities to minimize risk. By spreading investments, losses in one area can be offset by gains in others.

2. Options Hedging:

Options provide investors the right, but not the obligation, to buy or sell an asset (e.g., stocks) at a predetermined price within a specific time frame. By purchasing put options, investors can protect against potential losses during market downturns. Put options increase in value as the underlying asset declines, counteracting losses in the portfolio.

3. Long-Short Hedging:

This strategy involves simultaneously holding long positions (owning securities expected to go up in value) and short positions (selling borrowed securities, anticipating a decline). When executed correctly, gains from the short positions may alleviate losses from long positions during market corrections.

4. Pair Trading:

Pair trading involves taking simultaneous long and short positions in two related securities, such as two stocks within the same industry. The goal is to take advantage of relative over or undervaluation between the two stocks, irrespective of the broader market conditions.

Implementing Hedging Strategies:

To effectively implement hedging strategies during market corrections, investors should consider the following:

1. Assess Risk Tolerance:

Understanding your risk appetite is crucial in choosing appropriate hedging techniques. Determine how much of your portfolio you are comfortable hedging and the level of risk you are willing to bear.

2. Set Clear Objectives:

Define your investment objectives and align them with the appropriate hedging strategies. Whether it is capital preservation, downside protection, or maintaining portfolio growth, tailor your approach accordingly.

3. Regular Portfolio Evaluation:

Continuously reassess your portfolio's risk profile, asset allocation, and the effectiveness of employed hedging strategies. Adjustments may be necessary as market conditions evolve.

4. Seek Professional Advice:

Consider consulting a financial advisor or investment professional who can provide valuable insights into hedging strategies and their implementation based on your specific needs and market circumstances.

Conclusion:

Market corrections pose risks, but they also present opportunities for proactive investors to protect and grow their investments. Hedging is a powerful technique that can serve as a vital strategic tool during such market downturns. By implementing a well-rounded approach to hedging, diversifying portfolios, and employing various strategies, investors can navigate market corrections with greater confidence, ensuring the long-term preservation and growth of their investments.

17

Stop Loss Orders

A stop loss order is a tool used by investors to limit potential losses in a declining market. It functions as an automated instruction, directing a broker or trading platform to sell a specific security when its price drops to a predetermined level. This predetermined level, known as the stop price, is set by the investor based on their risk tolerance and investment objectives. Once the stop price is breached, the stop loss order is triggered, and the security is sold, mitigating further losses.

Strategies to Protect Investments using Stop Loss Orders:

1. Setting Appropriate Stop Loss Levels:

Careful consideration is essential when determining stop loss levels. Setting them too tight may lead to premature selling during normal market volatility. Conversely, setting them too loose may result in significant losses. Investors must assess their risk tolerance, investment horizon, and specific circumstances to determine appropriate levels.

2. Trailing Stop Loss Orders:

Trailing stop loss orders are dynamic stop prices that automatically adjust as the stock price increases. By using trailing stop loss orders, investors can protect their profits while maintaining the potential for further gains. These orders are particularly useful during times of volatility when rapid price fluctuations can occur.

3. Diversification:

Building a diversified investment portfolio can help protect against market corrections. By spreading investments across different asset classes, sectors, and geographical regions, investors can mitigate the impact of downturns in any one area. Diversification helps reduce risk by ensuring that losses in one investment can be offset by gains in others.

4. Regular Monitoring and Adjustments:

Markets can be unpredictable, and conditions can change rapidly. It is crucial for investors to regularly monitor their investments and make necessary adjustments to stop loss orders as market conditions evolve. Being proactive and responsive can help protect investments and maximize returns.

5. Consider Expert Advice:

For novice investors or those lacking confidence in their decision-making, seeking guidance from financial advisors or experts can be highly beneficial. These professionals can provide insights, assess risk tolerance, and help devise appropriate strategies tailored to individual investment goals.

Conclusion:

Market corrections can pose a significant challenge for investors. By implementing strategies to protect investments, such as the use of stop loss orders, investors can effectively manage risk and minimize losses during downturns. It is essential to understand the principles behind stop loss orders and combine them with other strategies like diversification, frequent monitoring, and seeking expert advice. By doing so, investors can navigate market corrections with confidence and increase their chances of long-term investment success.

V

Strategies to Grow Investments during Market Corrections

18

Overview

To effectively navigate market corrections and make the most of the situation, investors can employ various strategies. Here are some key strategies to grow investments during market corrections:

1. Dollar-Cost Averaging:

Dollar-cost averaging is a strategy where you consistently invest a fixed amount of money at regular intervals, regardless of market conditions. This technique takes advantage of market corrections by allowing you to buy more shares at lower prices. Over time, as the market recovers, your average cost per share can decrease, leading to potential gains in the long run.

2. Value Investing:

Market corrections often present buying opportunities for value investors. This strategy involves identifying fundamentally sound investments that are temporarily undervalued due to market sentiment. By thoroughly researching and analyzing companies' financials, competitive advantages, and growth prospects, investors can find bargains during downturns and potentially profit when the market recovers.

3. Rebalancing:

Regularly rebalancing your portfolio can be an effective strategy during market corrections. Rebalancing involves adjusting your asset allocation back to its original target allocation. For example, if the equity portion of your portfolio declines during a correction, you may need to sell some bonds and buy more stocks to maintain your desired balance. Rebalancing allows you to take advantage of lower prices and ensure that your portfolio aligns with your long-term goals.

4. Patience and Long-Term Perspective:

It is important to keep a long-term perspective during market corrections. Trying to time the market or make short-term moves based on market fluctuations can be risky. Instead, focus on solid investment fundamentals, stay patient, and stay invested. History has shown that markets eventually recover and continue to grow in the long run.

In conclusion, market corrections can be regarded as opportunities rather than threats. By employing strategies like diversification, asset allocation, dollar-cost averaging, value investing, rebalancing, and maintaining a long-term perspective, investors can protect their investments and potentially realize growth during market downturns. Seeking guidance from a financial advisor or investment professional is also advised to tailor these strategies to individual circumstances and goals.

19

Value Investing

Value investing strategies provide an opportunity to protect and grow investments during market corrections. This chapter will explore the concept of
market corrections, explain the principles of value investing, and delve into
strategies for effectively navigating market corrections.

1. Understanding Market Corrections:

- Market corrections occur when asset prices decline by approximately 10-20%
from their recent highs.

- Corrections are driven by various factors such as economic indicators,
geopolitical events, investor sentiment, or overvaluation.

- Market corrections are temporary and can be followed by recoveries and
subsequent market growth.

2. Introduction to Value Investing:

- Value investing is a long-term investment strategy that involves identifying
undervalued assets or stocks within the market.

- The central principle of value investing is to purchase investments at a price below their intrinsic value.

- Value investors focus on the fundamentals of an investment, such as earnings, assets, and future prospects, rather than short-term market fluctuations.

3. Strategies for Growing Investments During Market Corrections:

a. Evaluate and Diversify:

- Conduct a thorough evaluation of your investment portfolio to identify stocks or assets with sound fundamentals that may have been temporarily affected by the correction.

- Diversify your portfolio by investing across different sectors, industries, and asset classes to minimize risk and increase potential returns.

b. Buy Low, Sell High:

- Market corrections provide an opportunity to purchase quality assets or stocks at discounted prices.

- Value investors take advantage of these market downturns and buy into undervalued assets while holding onto existing investments.

- Selling investments during market corrections is generally discouraged unless there is a significant change in the intrinsic value of the investment.

c. Stick to Your Investment Strategy:

- Stay calm and committed to your long-term investment strategy, even during periods of market volatility.

- Avoid making impulsive decisions based on short-term market movements, as this can lead to potential losses.

- Patience and discipline in adhering to your investment plan are key to success in value investing during market corrections.

d. Regularly Monitor and Rebalance:

- Regularly review your investment portfolio to assess whether any adjustments are necessary.

- Rebalance your portfolio periodically to ensure your asset allocation aligns with your investment goals and risk tolerance.

- Take advantage of any opportunities that market corrections present by reallocating funds into undervalued assets.

Conclusion:

Market corrections are a natural part of financial markets, and value investing offers investors a framework to navigate these fluctuations. By identifying and investing in undervalued assets during market corrections, investors can potentially protect and grow their investments over the long term. Remember to exercise patience, diversify your portfolio, stick to your investment strategy, and regularly monitor and rebalance your investments to optimize your chances of success.

20

Dollar-Cost Averaging

Dollar-cost averaging, helps investors systematically invest over time, potentially lowering the average cost per share and mitigating risk. This chapter will provide an extensive overview of dollar-cost averaging as a strategy to grow investments during market corrections.

1. Understanding Market Corrections:

Before delving into strategies, it is essential to understand market corrections. Corrections are generally short-term declines in the market, typically characterized by a drop of around 10% to 20%. Investors should avoid panicking during a correction, as they are normal, healthy parts of market cycles.

2. The Concept of Dollar-Cost Averaging:

Dollar-cost averaging (DCA) is a strategy that involves investing a fixed amount of money at regular intervals, regardless of the market's performance. By consistently investing a set amount, investors buy more shares when prices are low and fewer shares when prices are high, potentially reducing the impact of market volatility and improving the overall investment performance.

3. How Dollar-Cost Averaging Works:

DCA works by spreading investments out over time, minimizing the risk associated with investing a lump sum at a single point in time. Investors establish a regular investment schedule, such as monthly or quarterly, and commit to investing a fixed amount during each period, irrespective of market conditions. Over time, this approach can lead to accumulating more shares at lower prices, resulting in better potential long-term returns.

4. Benefits of Dollar-Cost Averaging During Market Corrections:

i. Reduced Risk: DCA allows investors to mitigate the impact of short-term market volatility by buying stocks at different price points. This reduces the risk of investing a bulk amount at a market peak, potentially leading to significant losses.

ii. Emotionally Detached Investing: Regular investments through DCA enforce discipline, reducing the temptation to time the market based on emotions or short-term fluctuations.

iii. Lower Average Cost: Due to the varying stock prices during market corrections, DCA allows investors to buy shares at both high and low prices. Over time, this strategy lowers the average cost per share, potentially increasing potential gains.

5. Implementing Dollar-Cost Averaging:

Investors can typically implement DCA through the following steps:

i. Set a timeframe: Determine the period over which you plan to invest, such as a year or multiple years.

ii. Determine the investment amount: Decide how much you are comfortable investing at regular intervals.

iii. Set a schedule: Establish a regular investment schedule, for example, monthly or quarterly.

iv. Select investment vehicles: Choose the specific investments, such as mutual funds, index funds, or Exchange-Traded Funds (ETFs), depending on your risk tolerance and financial goals.

v. Monitor and review: Continuously assess your investment strategy and make adjustments as needed.

Conclusion:

Navigating market corrections requires a strategic approach to protect and grow investments. Dollar-cost averaging is a prudent strategy that allows investors to systematically invest during market downturns, potentially reducing risk and improving long-term performance. By implementing DCA, investors can embrace market corrections as potential buying opportunities, rather than solely focusing on short-term fluctuations, ultimately enhancing their investment journey.

21

Investing in Defensive Stocks

By understanding the concept of defensive stocks and implementing effective investment strategies, investors can protect their investments and potentially achieve long-term growth even during market downturns. This chapter aims to provide a comprehensive overview of strategies to grow investments by investing in defensive stocks within the context of market corrections.

1. Understanding Market Corrections:

Market corrections are temporary declines in stock prices that occur as a result of factors such as economic downturns, geopolitical tensions, or unexpected events. Corrections are considered normal and healthy for the overall market, acting as a balancing mechanism. Recognizing the potential impact of market corrections on investments is crucial for safeguarding and enhancing portfolio value.

2. Defensive Stocks:

Defensive stocks are stocks of companies that are less susceptible to economic cycles. They typically belong to industries that offer products or services that remain in demand regardless of the economic climate. Key characteristics of defensive stocks include stable earnings, consistent dividends, and limited vulnerability to market volatility. Companies operating in sectors like consumer staples, healthcare, utilities, and telecommunications often fall under this category.

3. Diversify Your Portfolio:

One of the fundamental strategies to reduce risk during market corrections is diversification. By building a well-diversified portfolio, investors can mitigate the impact of a downturn in one sector or asset class. Invest in a mix of defensive stocks alongside other stocks, bonds, real estate, and other assets that suit your risk tolerance and objectives.

4. Conduct Thorough Research:

Before investing in defensive stocks, conduct thorough research to identify strong companies that have a history of weathering market downturns. Analyze financial statements, earnings growth, dividend history, and market position. Look for companies with a competitive advantage, strong management teams, and a proven track record of adapting to changing market conditions.

5. Focus on Dividend-Paying Stocks:

Dividend-paying defensive stocks can provide a steady income stream and act as a cushion during market downturns. Companies that consistently pay dividends and have a history of increasing dividend payouts can offer attractive returns even when stock prices are lagging. Dividends can be reinvested to acquire additional shares, compounding portfolio growth over time.

6. Routinely Review and Rebalance:

Investors must actively review and rebalance their portfolios periodically, especially during market corrections. Regularly assess the performance of defensive stocks held within the portfolio and make adjustments as needed. This ensures the portfolio remains aligned with investment goals and risk tolerance.

7. Dollar-Cost Averaging:

Dollar-cost averaging involves investing a fixed amount of money into a particular security at regular intervals, regardless of market conditions. During market corrections, this strategy allows investors to purchase more shares at lower prices, potentially increasing long-term returns. As market conditions improve, the value of the overall investment may rise substantially.

8. Adopt a Long-Term Perspective:

Market corrections are temporary, and panic-driven decisions can often lead to suboptimal outcomes. By keeping a long-term perspective, investors can potentially ride out market downturns and capitalize on the eventual recovery. Maintaining a disciplined approach aligned with a sound investment plan is paramount for long-term success.

Conclusion:

Market corrections can be unsettling, but they also bring opportunities to enhance portfolio value. By investing in defensive stocks, diversifying across asset classes, conducting thorough research, focusing on dividends, and regularly reviewing and rebalancing, investors can strategically grow their investments during market corrections. Remember, a long-term perspective paired with a disciplined investment strategy can help safeguard and maximize returns during turbulent market phases.

VI

Role of Investment Advisors during Market Corrections

22

Overview

The role of investment advisors during market corrections plays a crucial part in helping individuals protect and grow their investments. Market corrections are periods of time when the overall stock market experiences a temporary downturn or decline in prices. These corrections can be unnerving for investors, as they often lead to a fluctuation in the value of their investments.

Investment advisors are professionals who specialize in providing guidance and recommendations relating to investment strategies. During market corrections, they become even more essential as they assist investors in navigating these turbulent times. Here are some key aspects of their role and how they can help:

1. Emotion management:

Investment advisors play a crucial role in managing emotions during market corrections. Many investors panic and make hasty decisions, such as selling stocks in a state of fear. Advisors provide a calm and rational perspective, reminding investors that market corrections are a normal part of the market cycle and advising against impulsive actions that may harm long-term financial goals.

2. Portfolio analysis:

Advisors assess individual investment portfolios to determine how they are positioned within the broader market. They review asset allocation, diversification, and risk tolerance levels to identify areas that may be particularly vulnerable during a market correction. By analyzing the overall composition of the portfolio, advisors can recommend adjustments to mitigate risk and minimize potential losses.

3. Risk management:

Investment advisors are skilled at assessing risk levels and implementing strategies to manage risk during market corrections. They may recommend diversification by spreading investments across different asset classes or sectors, reducing exposure to highly volatile stocks, or increasing holdings in defensive sectors. By adjusting the risk profile of an investment portfolio, advisors aim to protect against significant losses during market downturns.

4. Investment strategy adjustments:

Advisors work closely with investors to develop personalized investment strategies that align with their financial goals. During market corrections, these strategies may need to be adjusted. Advisors help determine whether a particular correction is temporary or indicative of a larger market trend. Based on this assessment, they may advise on changes to investment allocations, moving funds into safer assets such as bonds or cash equivalents, or seizing buying opportunities presented by undervalued stocks.

5. Opportunity identification:

Market corrections also provide opportunities for investors, and investment advisors are adept at recognizing such opportunities. They can identify sectors or companies that are likely to bounce back after the correction, allowing investors to take advantage of potential market upswings. Advisors keep a close eye on market trends, economic indicators, and valuation metrics to pinpoint these opportunities and recommend appropriate investment actions.

6. Disciplined approach:

One of the most valuable aspects of investment advisors during market corrections is their ability to instill discipline in investors. They emphasize the importance of staying focused on long-term goals, maintaining a diversified portfolio, and adhering to a predetermined investment strategy. Advisors provide ongoing support and accountability, preventing investors from making impulsive decisions based on short-term market volatilities.

In conclusion, investment advisors play a vital role during market corrections by assisting investors in safeguarding their investments and capitalizing on potential opportunities. Their expertise in emotion management, portfolio analysis, risk management, investment strategy adjustments, opportunity identification, and maintaining discipline can help individuals protect and grow their wealth in the face of market uncertainties.

23

Identifying Investment Opportunities

This chapter will discuss the role investment advisors play during market corrections, with a focus on identifying investment opportunities to mitigate risks and achieve long-term growth.

Understanding Market Corrections:

A market correction occurs when the market experiences a decline of at least 10% from its recent peak. Corrections can be triggered by various factors, including economic indicators, political events, or investor sentiment. It is important to note that market corrections are a normal part of market cycles and can provide potential investment opportunities.

The Role of Investment Advisors:

1. Risk Management:

Investment advisors play a crucial role in managing risk during market corrections. They analyze market data, evaluate economic conditions, and assess clients' risk profiles to develop a diversified investment strategy. By diversifying investments across different asset classes and regions, advisors aim to minimize the impact of market downturns on clients' portfolios.

2. Investment Research:

Investment advisors conduct extensive research to identify investment opportunities during market corrections. They examine various sectors, industries, and individual companies to determine undervalued assets that may have long-term growth potential. Through fundamental analysis, they evaluate financial health, management performance, competitive positioning, and other relevant factors to make informed investment recommendations.

3. Asset Allocation:

A critical aspect of an investment advisor's role during market corrections is adjusting asset allocation. Advisors may recommend shifting investments to less volatile asset classes, such as fixed income or defensive stocks, to preserve capital during market downturns. They also consider strategic positioning, rebalancing portfolios to take advantage of potential market upturns.

4. Buying Opportunities:

Market corrections often present buying opportunities for investors with a long-term perspective. Investment advisors actively seek these opportunities, identifying undervalued assets that could provide substantial returns over time. By leveraging their expertise and research, advisors guide their clients in making strategic investment decisions during market downturns.

5. Emotional Support:

Market corrections can cause anxiety and uncertainty among investors. Investment advisors provide emotional support by educating clients about market cycles and long-term investment strategies. They help clients navigate through emotional biases, encouraging discipline and rational decision-making during volatile market conditions.

Conclusion:

Investment advisors have a crucial role in guiding clients through market corrections. They provide risk management, research-based investment recommendations, asset allocation adjustments, and help investors capitalize on buying opportunities. By analyzing market trends and identifying under-valued assets, advisors aim to protect and grow clients' investments even in challenging market conditions. Remember, working with a knowledgeable investment advisor can provide you with the guidance and expertise needed to navigate market corrections while positioning your portfolio for long-term growth.

24

Managing Risks

One primary responsibility of investment advisors during market corrections is to provide guidance to their clients. They analyze market trends, monitor economic indicators, and evaluate the impact of various factors on investment portfolios. By staying informed about the market conditions, advisors can guide their clients through the turbulent times of market corrections.

A crucial aspect of managing risks during market corrections is diversification. Investment advisors recommend diversifying portfolios by allocating assets across different investment classes, such as stocks, bonds, real estate, and commodities. This diversification strategy helps reduce the overall risk exposure, as losses in one asset class are offset by gains in others.

Another strategy utilized by investment advisors is conducting thorough research and due diligence. They constantly review investment holdings, analyze company financials, and evaluate market opportunities to identify potential risks and make informed investment decisions. By being diligent and well-informed, investment advisors can help their clients navigate the uncertainties of market corrections.

During market corrections, investment advisors also engage in active portfolio management. They closely monitor market movements and adjust investment allocations accordingly. This involves reallocating assets, rebalancing portfolios, and making tactical moves to protect investments and seize opportunities that arise during market corrections. These active management strategies help optimize risk-adjusted returns and enhance long-term growth potential.

Moreover, investment advisors act as a source of emotional support for their clients during market corrections. The volatility and uncertainty can lead to panic-selling or irrational decisions, which may adversely impact investment outcomes. Advisors provide reassurance, rationalize market movements, and remind clients about the importance of sticking to their long-term investment plans. This helps prevent hasty decisions driven by emotional responses and ensures clients stay focused on their financial goals.

In summary, investment advisors perform a vital role during market corrections by managing risks and guiding their clients through turbulent times. They provide expertise in diversification, research, due diligence, and active portfolio management to safeguard investments and capitalize on opportunities. Additionally, they offer emotional support to prevent emotional decision-making. By leveraging their knowledge and experience, investment advisors help protect and grow the investments of individuals during market corrections.

25

Developing a Correction-Ready Portfolio

Investment advisors play a significant role in developing a correction-ready portfolio. In this chapter, we will explore the importance of investment advisors during market corrections and how they can assist in safeguarding and maximizing your investments.

Understanding Market Corrections:

Before delving into the role of investment advisors, it is crucial to comprehend market corrections. Market corrections are temporary reversals in a market trend, usually characterized by a decline of 10% or more from a recent peak. They can occur within a specific sector, asset class, or affect the entire market. While corrections can bring uncertainty and unease, they also create opportunities for investors to reposition their portfolios strategically.

The Role of Investment Advisors:

1. Objective Analysis:

Investment advisors bring an objective view to investment decisions during market corrections. Using their expertise and experience, they analyze market trends, economic data, and underlying factors influencing market behavior. By providing a well-informed perspective, advisors help investors make decisions based on facts rather than emotions.

2. Portfolio Review and Diversification:

During market corrections, investment advisors review and assess the existing portfolios of their clients. They ensure that the portfolio is diversified across various investment types, such as equities, bonds, cash equivalents, and alternative investments. Diversification helps reduce risk and potentially protect against substantial losses during corrections.

3. Risk Assessment and Management:

Investment advisors evaluate the risk tolerance and investment objectives of their clients. By understanding clients' risk preferences, advisors can adjust portfolio allocations accordingly. During market corrections, they may suggest allocating more capital to defensive sectors or asset classes that historically perform well during downturns, such as bonds or gold.

4. Maintaining a Long-Term Perspective:

One of the most valuable roles of investment advisors during market corrections is providing clients with reassurance and maintaining a long-term perspective. Advisors help clients resist the temptation to react emotionally to short-term market movements, reminding them of their investment goals and the advantages of staying invested for the long haul.

5. Identifying Investment Opportunities:

Market corrections often offer attractive buying opportunities. Investment advisors leverage their knowledge and research capabilities to identify under-valued assets or sectors that have strong growth potential. They help clients capitalize on these opportunities, potentially enhancing their investment returns when the market recovers.

Developing a Correction-Ready Portfolio:

Investment advisors play a crucial role in developing a correction-ready portfolio that can withstand market downturns. They consider various factors to craft a tailored portfolio, including:

1. Asset Allocation:

Advisors assist in determining the optimal mix of asset classes that align with clients' risk tolerance, investment goals, and time horizon. This helps to reduce the impact of market corrections on the overall portfolio.

2. Diversification:

Advisors ensure portfolios are well-diversified, spreading investments across multiple sectors, industries, and geographic regions. This diversification mitigates the risk of significant losses if one sector suffers during a market correction.

3. Regular Portfolio Review:

Investment advisors periodically review portfolios to ensure they remain aligned with clients' evolving needs and changing market conditions. They rebalance portfolios, making adjustments whenever required to maintain appropriate asset allocations.

4. Education and Communication:

Advisors enable clients to understand the intricacies of market corrections, providing educational resources and regular communication. This empowers clients to make well-informed decisions.

Conclusion:

In the volatile world of financial markets, investment advisors play a vital role in constructing correction-ready portfolios. By providing objective analysis, diversifying investments, managing risks, maintaining a long-term perspective, and identifying investment opportunities, advisors help investors protect and grow their investments during market corrections. Collaborating with a knowledgeable investment advisor can provide investors with peace of mind, ensuring their portfolios are positioned to withstand the unavoidable fluctuations of the market.

VII

Psychological Aspects of Market Corrections

26

Overview

Market corrections are inevitable in the world of investing, and understanding their psychological aspects is crucial for investors to protect and grow their investments. This chapter will provide a simple and extensive overview of the psychological aspects of market corrections.

1. Market Corrections Defined:

A market correction refers to a temporary reversal in the overall trend of a financial market, usually resulting in a decline of 10% or more. It is important to note that corrections are a natural part of market cycles and offer opportunities for investors as well as inherent risks.

2. Emotional Roller Coaster:

During market corrections, investors often experience a roller coaster of emotions. Fear, anxiety, and uncertainty tend to dominate, leading to irrational decision-making. Understanding these emotional drivers is essential in order to remain level-headed.

3. Loss Aversion and Risk Tolerance:

Loss aversion, the psychological bias where individuals prefer avoiding losses to acquiring gains, can significantly impact decision-making during market corrections. Investors must assess their risk tolerance and acknowledge that market fluctuations are a normal part of investing, which can help minimize impulsive actions.

4. Cognitive Biases:

Numerous cognitive biases can influence our judgment during market corrections. These biases include the availability bias (giving greater weight to recent events), confirmation bias (seeking information that aligns with pre-existing beliefs), and herd mentality (following the crowd). Recognizing these biases can help investors make more rational decisions.

5. Overcoming Emotional Challenges:

To protect and grow investments during market corrections, investors need to implement strategies to overcome emotional challenges. This may involve establishing a well-diversified portfolio, setting realistic long-term goals, and adopting a disciplined investment approach. Engaging with a financial advisor can also prove beneficial in navigating emotional challenges.

6. Behavioral Finance:

Behavioral finance, a field that merges psychology and finance, offers insights into irrational investor behavior during market corrections. Understanding concepts such as prospect theory, anchoring, and mental accounting can help investors make better decisions during turbulent market conditions.

7. Staying Informed:

During market corrections, staying informed yet discerning is crucial. Over-consumption of financial news or excessive monitoring of investment portfolios can heighten anxiety and increase the likelihood of making impulsive decisions. Focus on quality information from trusted sources and avoid excessive reliance on speculative news or social media.

8. Adopting a Long-Term Mindset:

In times of market corrections, it is vital to maintain a long-term perspective. Historically, markets have always recovered from corrections and continued their upward trajectory. Recognizing this fact can help investors avoid knee-jerk reactions and stay focused on their investment goals.

Conclusion:

The psychological aspects of market corrections play a significant role in how investors handle and navigate stormy financial markets. By understanding and managing emotions, overcoming cognitive biases, and adopting a disciplined approach based on sound financial principles, investors can protect and grow their investments even amidst market corrections. Remember, successful investing is as much about mindset as it is about financial knowledge and strategy.

27

Investor Behavior during Corrections

Corrections can be unsettling for investors, as they often experience a sense of uncertainty and anxiety about their investments.

Understanding the psychological aspects of market corrections is essential for investors who want to protect and grow their investments. Here are some key points to consider:

1. Fear and Greed:

The emotions of fear and greed frequently drive investor behavior during corrections. When the market is in decline, fear can cause some investors to panic and sell their investments in a hurry, sometimes resulting in substantial losses. On the other hand, greed can lead investors to take on excessive risks during periods of growth, which can come back to haunt them during market corrections.

2. Loss Aversion:

Psychologically, investors tend to feel the pain of losses more intensely than the pleasure of gains. This concept, known as loss aversion, can lead investors to make irrational decisions during corrections. They may be more inclined to focus on the potential loss of their investments rather than considering the potential for long-term growth.

3. Herd Mentality:

The fear and uncertainty of market corrections can trigger a herd mentality among investors. This behavior refers to the tendency of individuals to follow the actions of the majority, even if it may not be in their best interest. During corrections, when many investors start selling their positions, others may feel pressured to do the same, creating a negative feedback loop that further fuels the decline.

4. Overconfidence Bias:

Overconfidence bias is another psychological aspect that influences investor behavior during corrections. Some investors may believe they have superior knowledge or trading abilities that allow them to outperform the market consistently. As a result, they may underestimate the risks associated with corrections and fail to take appropriate precautions to protect their investments.

5. Time Horizon:

One's time horizon can significantly influence their behavior during market corrections. Long-term investors with a solid understanding of market cycles and a clear investment plan are more likely to stay the course and view corrections as potential buying opportunities. In contrast, short-term traders or investors with immediate financial objectives may feel more compelled to exit the market during corrections to prevent further losses.

6. Behavioral Biases:

Investors are prone to various behavioral biases that can impact their decision-making during market corrections. These biases include confirmation bias (seeking information that confirms existing beliefs), anchoring bias (relying too heavily on initial information), and availability bias (placing greater importance on information that is easily accessible). Becoming aware of these biases is crucial to making more rational investment decisions.

In summary, understanding the psychological aspects of investor behavior during market corrections is essential for protecting and growing investments. Recognizing common biases, managing emotions, and implementing sound investment strategies can help investors navigate market corrections with confidence and optimize their long-term financial goals.

28

Handling Fear and Greed

As investors navigate through market corrections, understanding the psychological factors that come into play, such as fear and greed, is crucial for making rational and informed decisions. In this chapter, we will explore the psychological aspects of market corrections and delve into strategies to effectively handle fear and greed to safeguard and enhance your investments.

I. Understanding Market Corrections:

A. Definition and Characteristics of Market Corrections
   B. Causes of Market Corrections
   C. Historical Examples of Market Corrections

II. Psychological Factors in Market Corrections:

A. Fear:

1. Role of Loss Aversion: Examining how investors are more driven by the fear of losing money than the potential for gains.

2. Impact of Confirmation Bias: Exploring how investors tend to seek information that aligns with their pre-existing beliefs, leading to irrational

decision-making during market corrections.

3. Herd Mentality and Fear of Missing Out (FOMO): Analyzing how fear can prompt investors to make impulsive investment decisions, driven by the fear of missing out on potential gains or being left behind.

B. Greed:

1. Role of Overconfidence Bias: Discussing how investors can become overconfident in their ability to predict market movements, leading to excessive risk-taking during bullish periods.

2. Chasing High Returns: Examining the tendency to prioritize short-term gains over long-term stability, potentially increasing vulnerability to market corrections.

3. Impact of Anchoring Bias: Discussing how investors often anchor their decisions based on past successes or popular investment trends, making them susceptible to greed-driven strategies during market upswings.

III. Strategies for Handling Fear and Greed during Market Corrections:

A. Educating and Preparing Yourself:

1. Understanding Your Risk Tolerance: Assessing your personal risk appetite to determine an appropriate investment strategy aligned with your goals.

2. Monitoring your Emotional State: Recognizing the emotional impact of market corrections and developing techniques to remain rational and calm.

B. Diversification and Asset Allocation:

1. Spreading Your Investments: Exploring the benefits of diversifying your

portfolio across different asset classes, industries, and geographic regions to mitigate risk.

2. Rebalancing: Discussing the importance of periodically assessing and adjusting your portfolio to maintain an appropriate asset allocation.

C. Long-term Investment Approach:

1. Avoiding Timing the Market: Emphasizing the difficulty of accurately predicting market movements and highlighting the benefits of a long-term investment strategy.

2. Dollar-Cost Averaging: Exploring the concept of investing a fixed amount at regular intervals, reducing the impact of short-term market fluctuations.

D. Seeking Professional Advice:

1. Utilizing the Expertise of Financial Advisors: Discussing the advantages of consulting with experienced professionals to help navigate market corrections.

Conclusion:

Navigating market corrections successfully requires a deep understanding of the psychological aspects involved, particularly the impact of fear and greed on investment decision-making. By recognizing these factors and employing effective strategies to handle fear and greed, investors can protect their investments and position themselves for long-term growth. Remember, knowledge and emotional discipline are key to making rational investment decisions during market corrections.

29

Importance of Patience and Discipline

This chapter focuses on the importance of patience and discipline during market corrections and aims to provide key insights on protecting and growing investments in these circumstances.

1. Understanding Market Corrections:

Market corrections are inevitable and occur due to various factors such as economic conditions, geopolitical events, or investor sentiment. They are typically short-term declines that reset stock prices to a more sustainable level. Recognizing that corrections are a normal part of market cycles is the first step in managing investor emotions.

2. Emotional Reactions:

During a market correction, emotions can run high, leading to impulsive decisions that may harm the investor's long-term financial goals. Common emotional reactions include fear, panic, and a desire to sell off investments. It is crucial to gain awareness of these emotions and keep them in check to avoid making irrational decisions.

3. The Importance of Patience:

Patience is a vital characteristic of successful investors, particularly during market corrections. It is essential to remember that corrections are temporary, and markets tend to recover over time. Being patient allows investors to weather the storm, avoid knee-jerk reactions, and let their investments grow over the long term.

4. Maintaining Discipline:

Discipline is another crucial psychological aspect when navigating market corrections. It involves following a well-defined investment strategy, sticking to predetermined asset allocation, and avoiding emotional responses driven by short-term market fluctuations. Discipline provides a rational framework for decision-making during periods of volatility.

5. Asset Allocation and Diversification:

Asset allocation and diversification play a significant role in managing expectations during market corrections. A well-diversified portfolio across various asset classes, such as stocks, bonds, and alternative investments, can help reduce the impact of market downturns on overall investment performance.

6. Long-Term Perspective:

Developing a long-term perspective is critical in the context of market corrections. Investors should focus on their investment horizon and long-term financial goals rather than trying to time the market or chase short-term gains. By looking beyond the immediate corrections, investors can stay focused on achieving long-term wealth accumulation.

7. Opportunities in Market Corrections:

Market corrections can also present opportunities for savvy investors. Prices of quality assets may become more attractive during market downturns, offer-ing opportunities to buy at discounted prices. Recognizing these opportunities requires a patient and disciplined approach to taking advantage of market volatility.

8. Professional Guidance:

Seeking professional guidance during market corrections can provide valuable insights and help investors make informed decisions. Financial advisors and investment professionals have experience in navigating difficult market conditions and can offer personalized strategies based on an individual's risk tolerance and financial goals.

Conclusion:

Understanding the psychological aspects of market corrections, along with the importance of patience and discipline, is paramount for investors looking to protect and grow their investments. By recognizing that market corrections are temporary and opportunities can arise during volatile times, investors can maintain a long-term perspective and make rational decisions aligned with their financial objectives. Patience and discipline serve as the bedrock for successful investing amid market corrections, allowing investors to weather short-term volatility and stay focused on their long-term wealth accumulation.

VIII

Legal and Regulatory Aspects of Market Corrections

30

Overview

Understanding the legal and regulatory aspects associated with market corrections is crucial for protecting and growing investments. This chapter will delve into the legal and regulatory considerations relevant to market corrections, providing valuable insights for investors seeking to navigate these challenging periods.

1. Investor Protection Measures:

During market corrections, regulators and governing bodies employ various measures to ensure investor protection. These mechanisms aim to maintain market integrity, prevent market manipulations, and provide investors with transparent information. Key investor protection measures include:

a. Disclosure and Reporting Obligations:

Companies listed on stock exchanges must disclose essential information to investors promptly, ensuring transparency in financial reporting. This helps investors make informed decisions during market corrections.

b. Insider Trading Regulations:

Securities laws prohibit insider trading, where individuals with access to privileged information exploit it for personal gain. These regulations protect ordinary investors during market fluctuations.

c. Securities Regulatory Bodies:

Regulatory bodies, such as the Securities and Exchange Commission (SEC) in the United States or the Financial Conduct Authority (FCA) in the United Kingdom, monitor markets, enforce regulations, and safeguard investor interests.

2. Securities Laws and Regulations:

Market corrections require investors to be mindful of various securities laws and regulations. Understanding these legal frameworks is essential for making sound investment decisions. Key areas to consider include:

a. Anti-Fraud Provisions:

Securities laws prohibit fraudulent activities, including misrepresentation, false statements, and misleading advertisements. These provisions maintain market integrity and protect investors during volatile market conditions.

b. Market Manipulation:

Manipulative practices, such as spreading false rumors, creating artificial demand/supply, or engaging in wash trades, are illegal. Regulatory bodies actively monitor and penalize individuals or entities involved in market manipulation, ensuring fair market practices.

c. Corporate Governance Regulations:

Companies are subject to specific corporate governance regulations, ensuring accountability, transparency, and fairness in decision-making. Investors should assess a company's corporate governance practices during market corrections to gauge potential risks.

3. Regulatory Responses to Market Corrections:

Regulatory bodies often intervene during market corrections to stabilize financial markets and mitigate risks. These responses may include:

a. Emergency Measures:

Regulators can implement emergency measures, such as circuit breakers or temporary trading halts, to manage extreme market volatility and prevent panic-driven selling or buying.

b. Economic Stimulus:

Governments and central banks may introduce economic stimulus measures, such as interest rate adjustments or fiscal policies, to stimulate economic growth during market downturns. These measures can influence market conditions, impacting investment decisions.

c. Enhanced Surveillance:

Regulatory bodies increase market surveillance during market corrections to detect and prevent market abuses, insider trading, and other illegal activities that could exacerbate volatility.

Conclusion:

Understanding the legal and regulatory aspects of market corrections is essential for investors looking to protect and grow their investments during periods of market uncertainty. Being aware of investor protection measures, securities laws, and regulatory responses allows investors to make well-informed decisions, navigate challenges, and capitalize on opportunities presented by market corrections. Engaging with financial advisors and staying updated on regulatory changes ensures investors remain knowledgeable and prepared for potential market fluctuations.

31

Government Interventions

Legal and regulatory frameworks are necessary to ensure market integrity, transparency, and investor protection during these challenging times. They provide guidelines and rules to prevent market manipulation, fraud, and unfair practices. Examples of such regulations include securities laws, exchange regulations, and rules regarding financial disclosures.

During market corrections, governments may intervene through various mechanisms to stabilize the markets and protect investors. Some common government interventions include:

1. Monetary Policy:

Central banks can adjust interest rates or implement quantitative easing measures to stimulate economic growth and provide liquidity to financial institutions. By reducing borrowing costs, they aim to encourage investments and consumer spending.

2. Regulatory Measures:

Governments may introduce temporary regulations or invoke existing laws to manage market turbulence. For example, they may impose restrictions on short-selling (the practice of betting against declining stock prices) to prevent excessive speculation during market downturns.

3. Investor Protection:

Governments have agencies and organizations responsible for safeguarding investor interests. These entities regulate financial institutions, enforce compliance with securities laws, and handle investor complaints. Their role is to ensure fair trading practices, prevent fraud, and promote transparency.

4. Bailouts and Stimulus Packages:

In more severe cases, governments may provide financial assistance to struggling industries, businesses, or financial institutions to prevent systemic risks and stabilize the overall economy. These measures aim to restore market confidence and prevent a deep and prolonged economic downturn.

5. Communication and Coordination:

Governments also play a vital role in communicating with the public during market corrections. Through transparent communication channels, they provide updates, guidance, and reassurance to investors, helping manage panic and restore confidence in the markets.

In conclusion, legal and regulatory aspects of market corrections and government interventions play a crucial role in maintaining stability and fairness in financial markets. Through appropriate regulations, government measures, and investor protection mechanisms, authorities aim to protect and grow investments, while ensuring transparency and market integrity. Understanding these aspects is essential for individuals seeking to safeguard their investments and navigate market uncertainties.

32

Regulatory Guidelines for Investors

This chapter will discuss the legal and regulatory guidelines established by financial authorities to assist investors in effectively navigating market corrections and mitigating potential risks.

I. Market Corrections:

A market correction refers to a temporary decline in the value of stocks, commodities, or other financial instruments after a period of significant growth. These corrections are a natural part of the market cycle, readjusting prices to a more sustainable level. Market corrections can be triggered by various factors such as economic indicators, geopolitical events, or shifts in investor sentiment.

II. Importance of Legal and Regulatory Aspects:

1. Investor Protection:

Regulatory guidelines aim to protect investors from fraudulent practices, manipulation, and unfair trading activities during market corrections. They provide a framework for maintaining market integrity and ensuring fair market practices.

2. Risk Mitigation:

By establishing guidelines, regulators seek to mitigate risks associated with market volatility. These guidelines highlight best practices for investors to safeguard their investments and make informed decisions during turbulent market conditions.

III. Regulatory Guidelines for Investors:

1. Disclosure Requirements:

Financial authorities typically require companies and financial institutions to disclose relevant information to investors promptly. During market corrections, these guidelines ensure that accurate and timely information is provided, enabling investors to assess the implications of market conditions on their investments.

2. Investor Education and Awareness:

Regulatory bodies emphasize the importance of investor education programs to enhance financial literacy and empower individuals to understand the risks and opportunities associated with market corrections. These programs educate investors on diversification, risk management, and the importance of long-term investment strategies.

3. Suitability and Appropriateness:

Financial regulations necessitate that investment advisors and brokers assess the suitability and appropriateness of investment products for individual investors. During market corrections, these guidelines ensure that advisors consider investors' risk tolerance, investment goals, and time horizons to offer appropriate recommendations.

4. Market Surveillance and Manipulation Prevention:

Regulatory bodies employ market surveillance tools to monitor trading activities and identify potential market manipulation during market corrections. These guidelines aim to maintain market fairness, transparency, and investor confidence.

5. Circuit Breakers and Temporary Halts:

Stock exchanges often implement circuit breakers or temporary halts in trading to counter extreme market volatility during corrections. These regulatory measures aim to prevent panic selling, maintain orderly markets, and provide investors with a brief pause for reevaluation.

IV. Regulatory Authorities:

Financial authorities such as the Securities and Exchange Commission (SEC) in the United States, the Financial Conduct Authority (FCA) in the United Kingdom, and similar regulatory bodies worldwide establish and enforce these legal and regulatory guidelines. These authorities continuously review and update regulations to adapt to changing market dynamics and protect investor interests.

In conclusion, understanding the legal and regulatory aspects of market corrections is crucial for investors looking to protect and grow their investments. These guidelines ensure investor protection, risk mitigation, and market stability during periods of market volatility. By adhering to these regulations, investors can navigate market corrections with prudence, make informed decisions, and foster long-term financial growth.

33

Legal Rights and Protections for Investors

This chapter aims to provide a comprehensive understanding of investor rights and protections in the context of market corrections.

1. Disclosure Requirements:

To ensure transparency and fairness, governments and regulatory bodies implement disclosure requirements that oblige companies to provide timely and accurate information concerning their financial results, operations, and risks. Publicly traded companies must disclose material information that could affect investors' decisions, including the disclosure of any material changes during market corrections that may impact stock prices.

2. Securities Laws and Regulations:

Securities laws are designed to protect investors and maintain the integrity of the financial markets. These laws establish regulations for trading and investments, aiming to prevent fraud, insider trading, market manipulation, and other illegal activities. Compliance with securities laws is a cornerstone for investor protection in the event of market corrections.

3. Investor Protection Agencies:

In many countries, government-backed agencies and regulatory bodies act as watchdogs to safeguard investors' interests. These agencies, such as the Securities and Exchange Commission (SEC) in the United States or Financial Conduct Authority (FCA) in the United Kingdom, oversee the enforcement of securities laws, regulate brokers and financial institutions, and provide information and resources for investors. Understanding the role and functions of these agencies can help investors navigate market corrections.

4. Investor Rights:

Investors have certain legal rights that protect their investments, even during market corrections. These rights may include the right to accurate and timely information, the right to a fair and efficient market, the right to legal recourse in case of fraud or misleading practices, and the right to vote on significant corporate decisions. It is crucial for investors to be aware of their rights and how they can exercise them in the event of market volatility.

5. Investor Protection Measures:

In addition to regulatory agencies, various measures exist to protect investors in times of market corrections. These measures may include investment insurance, such as the Securities Investor Protection Corporation (SIPC) in the United States, which provides limited protection in case of broker-dealer failures. Additionally, investment professionals, such as financial advisors, are required to adhere to certain fiduciary duties and ethical standards to ensure the well-being of their clients' investments.

6. Diversification and Risk Management:

While legal and regulatory aspects provide a safety net for investors, personal risk management strategies are also essential during market corrections. Diversifying investments across different asset classes, sectors, and geographical regions can reduce the impact of market downturns on a portfolio.

Moreover, employing risk management techniques, such as setting stop-loss orders or implementing trailing stops, can help limit potential losses in volatile market conditions.

Conclusion:

Market corrections are an inherent part of the investment landscape. Understanding the legal and regulatory aspects of market corrections is crucial for protecting investors' rights and investments. By being aware of disclosure requirements, securities laws, investor protection agencies, and personal risk management strategies, investors can navigate through market corrections with greater confidence and strive to preserve and grow their investments in the long term.

About the Author

Clara Capital is a pseudonym for an astute financial analyst with over a decade of experience in the world of finance and investment. With a keen eye for market trends and a passion for educating others, Clara has dedicated herself to helping investors navigate the ever-evolving economic landscape. Her insights are rooted in deep research and real-world experience, making her guidance both practical and invaluable. When she's not analyzing market shifts, Clara enjoys reading historical novels and exploring nature trails.